BOOKS BY W. S. GRAHAM

Cage Without Grievance (1942)

The Seven Journeys (1944)

2nd Poems (1945)

The White Threshold (1949)

The Nightfishing (1955)

Malcolm Mooney's Land (1970)

Implements in Their Places (1977)

SELECTED POEMS

W. S. Graham, 1918-

SELECTED

POEMS

The Ecco Press

NEW YORK

Copyright © 1979 by W. S. Graham

First published by The Ecco Press in 1980
1 West 30th Street, New York, N.Y. 10001
Printed in the United States of America
The Ecco Press logo by Ahmed Yacoubi
Cover design by Cynthia Krupat
This edition published by arrangement with Faber and Faber Ltd.
Library of Congress Cataloging in Publication Data
Graham, William Sydney, 1918–   /   Selected poems.
PR6013.R23A17   1980   821'.914   80-11534
ISBN 0-912-94673-3
ISBN 0-912-94674-1 pbk.

ACKNOWLEDGEMENTS

Acknowledgements are due to the following periodicals in which some of these poems have previously appeared:

Accent, Akros, Angry Penguins, Antaeus, Aquarius, Ariel, Best of the Poetry Year 6, Botteghe Oscure, Briarcliff Quarterly, Bugle Blast, Circle, Contemporary Poetry, The Cornish Review, Counterpoint, Cracked Looking Glass, Disco, Encounter, Experiment, Faber Scottish Anthology, Horizon, Hudson Review, Life and Letters, Lines Review, The Listener, The London Magazine, Malahat Review, Merlin, New British Poets, New Poems 1975, New Poetry, New Statesman, Nimbus, Now, Observer, Pembroke Magazine, Penguin Poets (with David Gascoyne and Kathleen Raine), *PN Review, Pocket Poetry, Poetry, Poetry London, Poetry Nation, Poetry Quarterly, Poetry Review, Poetry Scotland, Poetry St Ives, Quarterly Review of Literature, Scottish Review, Sewanee Review, Stand, The Times Literary Supplement, Voices, Wake, Windmill, Writing Today.*

The author wishes to thank the Arts Council for grants in the summers of 1969 and 1975.

CONTENTS

What Is The Language Using Us For? / 3

The Constructed Space / 9

Ten Shots Of Mister Simpson / 10

Five Visitors To Madron / 16

Malcolm Mooney's Land / 19

Listen. Put On Morning / 24

Approaches To How They Behave / 26

The Thermal Stair / 32

The Beast In The Space / 35

The Found Picture / 36

Lines on Roger Hilton's Watch / 38

Dear Bryan Wynter / 40

Baldy Bane / 43

Men Sign The Sea / 49

The Nightfishing / 50

Greenock At Night I Find You / 67

To Alexander Graham / 68

Johann Joachim Quantz's First Lesson / 70

The Narrator / 71

Explanation Of A Map / 73

Here Next The Chair I Was When Winter Went / 75

The Lying Dear / 76

Dear Who I Mean / 77

Letter IV / 79

Yours Truly / 83

Language Ah Now You Have Me / 85

I Leave This At Your Ear / 87

The Night City / 88

A Note To The Difficult One / 90

To My Wife At Midnight / 91

Implements In Their Places / 94

SELECTED POEMS

WHAT IS THE LANGUAGE USING US FOR?

First Poem

What is the language using us for?
Said Malcolm Mooney moving away
Slowly over the white language.
Where am I going said Malcolm Mooney.

Certain experiences seem to not
Want to go in to language maybe
Because of shame or the reader's shame.
Let us observe Malcolm Mooney.

Let us get through the suburbs and drive
Out further just for fun to see
What he will do. Reader, it does
Not matter. He is only going to be

Myself and for you slightly you
Wanting to be another. He fell
He falls (Tenses are everywhere.)
Deep down into a glass jail.

I am in a telephoneless, blue
Green crevasse and I can't get out.
I pay well for my messages
Being hoisted up when you are about.

I suppose you open them under the light
Of midnight of The Dancing Men.
The point is would you ever want
To be down here on the freezing line

Reading the words that steam out
Against the ice? Anyhow draw
This folded message up between
The leaning prisms from me below.

Slowly over the white language
Comes Malcolm Mooney the saviour.
My left leg has no feeling.
What is the language using us for?

Second Poem

I

What is the language using us for?
It uses us all and in its dark
Of dark actions selections differ.

I am not making a fool of myself
For you. What I am making is
A place for language in my life

Which I want to be a real place
Seeing I have to put up with it
Anyhow. What are Communication's

Mistakes in the magic medium doing
To us? It matters only in
So far as we want to be telling

Each other alive about each other
Alive. I want to be able to speak
And sing and make my soul occur

In front of the best and be respected
For that and even be understood
By the ones I like who are dead.

I would like to speak in front
Of myself with all my ears alive
And find out what it is I want.

2

What is the language using us for?
What shape of words shall put its arms
Round us for more than pleasure?

I met a man in Cartsburn Street
Thrown out of the Cartsburn Vaults.
He shouted Willie and I crossed the street

And met him at the mouth of the Close.
And this was double-breasted Sam,
A far relation on my mother's

West-Irish side. Hello Sam how
Was it you knew me and says he
I heard your voice on The Sweet Brown Knowe.

O was I now I said and Sam said
Maggie would have liked to see you.
I'll see you again I said and said

Sam I'll not keep you and turned
Away over the shortcut across
The midnight railway sidings.

What is the language using us for?
From the prevailing weather or words
Each object hides in a metaphor.

This is the morning. I am out
On a kind of Vlaminck blue-rutted
Road. Willie Wagtail is about.

In from the West a fine smirr
Of rain drifts across the hedge.
I am only out here to walk or

Make this poem up. The hill is
A shining blue macadam top.
I lean my back to the telegraph pole

And the messages hum through my spine.
The beaded wires with their birds
Above me are contacting London.

What is the language using us for?
It uses us all and in its dark
Of dark actions selections differ.

Third Poem

I

What is the language using us for?
The King of Whales dearly wanted
To have a word with me about how
I had behaved trying to crash
The Great Barrier. I could not speak
Or answer him easily in the white
Crystal of Art he set me in.

Who is the King of Whales? What is
He like? Well you may ask. He is
A kind of old uncle of mine
And yours mushing across the blind

Ice-cap between us in his furs
Shouting at his delinquent dogs.
What is his purpose? I try to find

Whatever it is is wanted by going
Out of my habits which is my name
To ask him how I can do better.
Tipped from a cake of ice I slid
Into the walrus-barking water
To find. I did not find another
At the end of my cold dry.

2

What is the language using us for?
The sailing men had sailing terms
Which rigged their inner-sailing thoughts
In forecastle and at home among
The kitchen of their kind. Tarry
Old Jack is taken aback at a blow
On the lubber of his domestic sea.

Sam, I had thought of going again
But it's no life. I signed on years
Ago and it wasn't the ship for me.
O leave 'er Johnny leave 'er.
Sam, what readers do we have aboard?
Only the one, Sir. Who is that?
Only myself, Sir, from Cartsburn Street.

3

What is the language using us for?
I don't know. Have the words ever
Made anything of you, near a kind

Of truth you thought you were? Me
Neither. The words like albatrosses
Are only a doubtful touch towards
My going and you lifting your hand

To speak to illustrate an observed
Catastrophe. What is the weather
Using us for where we are ready
With all our language lines aboard?
The beginning wind slaps the canvas.
Are you ready? Are you ready?

THE CONSTRUCTED SPACE

Meanwhile surely there must be something to say,
Maybe not suitable but at least happy
In a sense here between us two whoever
We are. Anyhow here we are and never
Before have we two faced each other who face
Each other now across this abstract scene
Stretching between us. This is a public place
Achieved against subjective odds and then
Mainly an obstacle to what I mean.

It is like that, remember. It is like that
Very often at the beginning till we are met
By some intention risen up out of nothing.
And even then we know what we are saying
Only when it is said and fixed and dead.
Or maybe, surely, of course we never know
What we have said, what lonely meanings are read
Into the space we make. And yet I say
This silence here for in it I might hear you.

I say this silence or, better, construct this space
So that somehow something may move across
The caught habits of language to you and me.
From where we are it is not us we see
And times are hastening yet, disguise is mortal.
The times continually disclose our home.
Here in the present tense disguise is mortal.
The trying times are hastening. Yet here I am
More truly now this abstract act become.

TEN SHOTS OF MISTER SIMPSON

1

Ah Mister Simpson shy spectator
This morning in our November,
Don't run away with the idea
You are you spectating me.

On the contrary from this hide
Under my black cloth I see
You through the lens close enough
For comfort. Yes slightly turn

Your head more to the right and don't
Don't blink your eyes against the rain.
I have I almost have you now.
I want the line of the sea in.

Now I have you too close up.
As a face your face has disappeared.
All I see from my black tent
Is on the shelf of your lower lid
A tear like a travelling rat.

2

The camera nudges him to scream
Silently into its face.
Silently his thought recalls
Across the side of Zennor Hill.

He is here only recalling
Himself being pointed at
By somebody ago and even not
Understanding the language.

I am to do him no harm.
Mister Simpson, stand still.
Look at him standing sillily
For our sake and for the sake
Of preservation. He imagines
Still he is going to be shot.

3

He is as real as you looking
Over my November shoulder.
The sky chimes and the slewing light
Comes over Zennor Hill striking
The white of his escaped head.
His face comes dazzling through the glass
Into my eye imprisoned by Art.
His wife is gone. He has a daughter
Somewhere. Shall I snap him now?
No, you take him and get the number
Now that he's rolled up his sleeves.

4

Mister Simpson Blakean bright
Exile in our Sunday morning,
Stand still get ready jump in your place
Lie down get up don't speak. Number?
Fear not. It is only the high Zennor
Kestrel and I have clicked the shutter.

5

This time I want your face trying
To not remember dear other
Numbers you left, who did not follow

Follow follow you into this kind
Of last home held below the Zennor
Bracken fires and hovering eye.
Move and turn your unpronounceable
Name's head to look at where the horse
Black in its meadow noses the stone.

6

And here I am today below
The hill invisible in mist
In impossible light knocking.
My subject does not expect me.

Mister Simpson, can I with my drenched
Eyes but not with weeping come in?
Five diminishing tureens hang
Answering the fire from the kitchen wall.
There is a dog lying with cataracting
Eyes under a table. The mantel's brasses
Make a bright gloom and in the corner
A narrow Kiev light makes an ikon.

And who would have it in verse but only
Yourself too near having come in only
To look over my shoulder to see
How it is done. You are wrong. You are wrong
Being here, but necessary. Somebody
Else must try to see what I see.

Mister Simpson, turn your face
To get the gold of the fire on it.
Keep still. I have you nearly now.

So I made that. I got in also
A His Master's Voice gramophone,

A jug of Sheepsbit Scabious and
A white-rigged ship bottled sailing
And the mantel-piece in focus with even
A photograph of five young gassed
Nephews and nieces fading brown.

7

Not a cloud, the early wide morning
Has us both in, me looking
And you looking. Come and stand.
Aloft the carn behind you moves
So slowly down to anciently
Remember men looking at men
As uneasily as us. Mister Simpson,
Forgive me. The whole high moor is moving
Down to keep us safe in its gaze
As looking-at-each-other beasts
Who suddenly fly running into
The lens from fearful, opposite sides.
Not a cloud, the early wide morning
Has us both in looking out.

8

Mister Simpson, kneedeep in the drowned
Thistles of not your own country,
What is your category? What number
Did you curl into alone to sleep
The cold away in Hut K
Fifty-five nearest God the Chimney?
Now I have you sighted far
Out of the blackthorn and the wired
Perimeter into this particular
No less imprisoned place. You shall

Emerge here within different
Encirclements in a different time
Where I can ask you to lean easily
Against the young ash at your door
And with your hand touch your face
And look through into my face and into
The gentle reader's deadly face.

9

Today below this buzzard hill
Of real weather manufactured
By me the wisps slide slowly
Over the cottage you stand courageously
Outside of with a spade in your hand.
Pretend the mist has come across
Straight from your own childhood gathering
Berries on a picnic. The mist
Is only yours, I see by your face.
I am charging you nothing, Mister
Simpson. Stand and look easily
Beyond me as you always do.
I have you now and you didn't even
Feel anything but I have killed you.

10

Ah Mister Simpson shy spectator
This morning in our November,
I focus us across the curving
World's edge to put us down
For each other into the ordinary
Weather to be seen together still.
Language, put us down for the last
Time under real Zennor Hill
Before it moves into cloud.

Ah Mister Simpson, Ah Reader, Ah
Myself, our pictures are being taken.
We stand still. Zennor Hill,
Language and light begin to go
To leave us looking at each other.

FIVE VISITORS TO MADRON

In the small hours on the other side
Of language with my chair drawn
Up to the frightening abstract
Table of silence, taps. A face
Of white feathers turns my head
To suddenly see between the mad
Night astragals her looking in
Or wanted this to happen. She
Monster muse old bag or. Something
Dreamed is yes you're welcome always
Desired to drop in. It was your bleached
Finger on the pane which startled me
Although I half-expected you
But not you as you are but whoever
Would have looked in instead, another
More to my liking, not so true.

He realized it was a mistake. Closing
The door of the tomb afterwards
Secretly he thanked whoever
He could imagine to thank, some quick
Thought up thankable god of the moment.

2

As slow as distant spray falling
On the nether rocks of a headland never
Encountered but through the eye, the first
Of morning's ghost in blue palely
Hoisted my reluctant lid.
Watch what you say I said and watched

The day I uttered taking shape
To hide me in its bright bosom.

Like struck flints black flocking jack
Daws wheel over the Madron roofs.

3

I am longing not really longing
For what dont tell me let me think.
Or else I have to settle for
That step is that a step outside
At my back a new eddy of air?
And left these words at a loss to know
What form stood watching behind me
Reading us over my shoulder. I said
Now that you have come to stand
There rank-breathed at my elbow I will
Not be put off. This message must
Reach the others without your help.

4

And met the growing gaze willing
To give its time to me to let
Itself exchange discernments
If that surely it said is what
I wanted. Quick panics put out
A field of images round me to
Look back out at it from and not
Be gazed out of all composure.
And found my research ridiculously
Ending forced to wear a mask
Of a held-up colander to peer
Through as the even gaze began

Slowly to abate never having asked
Me if I had recognized an old
Aspect of need there once my own.

Terror-spots itch on my face now.
My mind is busy hanging up
Back in their places imagination's
Clever utensils. I scratch my cheek.

5

When the fifth came I had barely drawn
A breath in to identify who
I newly am in my new old house
In Madron near the slaughterhouse.

The hint was as though a child running
Late for school cried and seemed
To have called my name in the morning
Hurrying and my name's wisp
Elongated. Leaves me here
Nameless at least very without
That name mine ever to be called
In that way different again.

MALCOLM MOONEY'S LAND

Today, Tuesday, I decided to move on
Although the wind was veering. Better to move
Than have them at my heels, poor friends
I buried earlier under the printed snow.
From wherever it is I urge these words
To find their subtle vents, the northern dazzle
Of silence cranes to watch. Footprint on foot
Print, word on word and each on a fool's errand.
Malcolm Mooney's Land. Elizabeth
Was in my thoughts all morning and the boy.
Wherever I speak from or in what particular
Voice, this is always a record of me in you.
I can record at least out there to the west
The grinding bergs and, listen, further off
Where we are going, the glacier calves
Making its sudden momentary thunder.
This is as good a night, a place as any.

2

From the rimed bag of sleep, Wednesday,
My words crackle in the early air.
Thistles of ice about my chin,
My dreams, my breath a ruff of crystals.
The new ice falls from canvas walls.
O benign creature with the small ear-hole,
Submerger under silence, lead
Me where the unblubbered monster goes
Listening and makes his play.
Make my impediment mean no ill
And be itself a way.

A fox was here last night (Maybe Nansen's,
Reading my instruments.) the prints
All round the tent and not a sound.
Not that I'd have him call my name.
Anyhow how should he know? Enough
Voices are with me here and more
The further I go. Yesterday
I heard the telephone ringing deep
Down in a blue crevasse.
I did not answer it and could
Hardly bear to pass.

Landlice, always my good bedfellows,
Ride with me in my sweaty seams.
Come bonny friendly beasts, brother
To the grammarsow and the word-louse,
Bite me your presence, keep me awake
In the cold with work to do, to remember
To put down something to take back.
I have reached the edge of earshot here
And by the laws of distance
My words go through the smoking air
Changing their tune on silence.

3

My friend who loves owls
Has been with me all day
Walking at my ear
And speaking of old summers
When to speak was easy.
His eyes are almost gone
Which made him hear well.
Under our feet the great
Glacier drove its keel.
What is to read there
Scored out in the dark?

Later the north-west distance
Thickened towards us.
The blizzard grew and proved
Too filled with other voices
High and desperate
For me to hear him more.
I turned to see him go
Becoming shapeless into
The shrill swerving snow.

4

Today, Friday, holds the white
Paper up too close to see
Me here in a white-out in this tent of a place
And why is it there has to be
Some place to find, however momentarily
To speak from, some distance to listen to?

Out at the far-off edge I hear
Colliding voices, drifted, yes
To find me through the slowly opening leads.
Tomorrow I'll try the rafted ice.
Have I not been trying to use the obstacle
Of language well? It freezes round us all.

5

Why did you choose this place
For us to meet? Sit
With me between this word
And this, my furry queen.
Yet not mistake this
For the real thing. Here
In Malcolm Mooney's Land

I have heard many
Approachers in the distance
Shouting. Early hunters
Skittering across the ice
Full of enthusiasm
And making fly and,
Within the ear, the yelling
Spear steepening to
The real prey, the right
Prey of the moment.
The honking choir in fear
Leave the tilting floe
And enter the sliding water.
Above the bergs the foolish
Voices are lighting lamps
And all their sounds make
This diary of a place
Writing us both in.

Come and sit. Or is
It right to stay here
While, outside the tent
The bearded blinded go
Calming their children
Into the ovens of frost?
And what's the news? What
Brought you here through
The spring leads opening?

Elizabeth, you and the boy
Have been with me often
Especially on those last
Stages. Tell him a story.
Tell him I came across
An old sulphur bear
Sawing his log of sleep
Loud beneath the snow.

He puffed the powdered light
Up on to this page
And here his reek fell
In splinters among
These words. He snored well.
Elizabeth, my furry
Pelted queen of Malcolm
Mooney's Land, I made
You here beside me
For a moment out
Of the correct fatigue.

I have made myself alone now.
Outside the tent endless
Drifting hummock crests.
Words drifting on words.
The real unabstract snow.

LISTEN. PUT ON MORNING

Listen. Put on morning.
Waken into falling light.
A man's imagining
Suddenly may inherit
The handclapping centuries
Of his one minute on earth.
And hear the virgin juries
Talk with his own breath
To the corner boys of his street.
And hear the Black Maria
Searching the town at night.
And hear the playropes caa
The sister Mary in.
And hear Willie and Davie
Among bracken of Narnain
Sing in a mist heavy
With myrtle and listeners.
And hear the higher town
Weep a petition of fears
At the poorhouse close upon
The public heartbeat.
And hear the children tig
And run with my own feet
Into the netting drag
Of a suiciding principle.
Listen. Put on lightbreak.
Waken into miracle.
The audience lies awake
Under the tenements
Under the sugar docks
Under the printed moments.
The centuries turn their locks
And open under the hill

Their inherited books and doors
All gathered to distil
Like happy berry pickers
One voice to talk to us.
Yes listen. It carries away
The second and the years
Till the heart's in a jacket of snow
And the head's in a helmet white
And the song sleeps to be wakened
By the morning ear bright.
Listen. Put on morning.
Waken into falling light.

APPROACHES TO HOW THEY BEHAVE

1

What does it matter if the words
I choose, in the order I choose them in,
Go out into a silence I know
Nothing about, there to be let
In and entertained and charmed
Out of their master's orders? And yet
I would like to see where they go
And how without me they behave.

2

Speaking is difficult and one tries
To be exact and yet not to
Exact the prime intention to death.
On the other hand the appearance of things
Must not be made to mean another
Thing. It is a kind of triumph
To see them and to put them down
As what they are. The inadequacy
Of the living, animal language drives
Us all to metaphor and an attempt
To organize the spaces we think
We have made occur between the words.

3

The bad word and the bad word and
The word which glamours me with some
Quick face it pulls to make me let
It leave me to go across

In roughly your direction, hates
To go out maybe so completely
On another silence not its own.

4

Before I know it they are out
Afloat in the head which freezes them.
Then I suppose I take the best
Away and leave the others arranged
Like floating bergs to sink a convoy.

5

One word says to its mate O
I do not think we go together
Are we doing any good here
Why do we find ourselves put down?
The mate pleased to be spoken to
Looks up from the line below
And says well that doubtful god
Who has us here is far from sure
How we on our own tickle the chin
Of the prince or the dame that lets us in.

6

The dark companion is a star
Very present like a dark poem
Far and unreadable just out
At the edge of this poem floating.
It is not more or less a dark
Companion poem to the poem.

Language is expensive if
We want to strut, busked out
Showing our best on silence.
Good Morning. That is a bonny doing
Of verbs you wear with the celandine
Catching the same sun as mine.
You wear your dress like a prince but
A country's prince beyond my ken.
Through the chinks in your lyric coat
My ear catches a royal glimpse
Of fuzzed flesh, unworded body.
Was there something you wanted to say?
I myself dress up in what I can
Afford on the broadway. Underneath
My overcoat of the time's slang
I am fashionable enough wearing
The grave-clothes of my generous masters.

8

And what are you supposed to say
I asked a new word but it kept mum.
I had secretly admired always
What I thought it was here for.
But I was wrong when I looked it up
Between the painted boards. It said
Something it was never very likely
I could fit in to a poem in my life.

9

The good word said I am not pressed
For time. I have all the foxglove day
And all my user's days to give
You my attention. Shines the red

Fox in the digitalis grove.
Choose me choose me. Guess which
Word I am here calling myself
The best. If you can't fit me in
To lying down here among the fox
Glove towers of the moment, say
I am yours the more you use me. Tomorrow
Same place same time give me a ring.

10

Backwards the poem's just as good.
We human angels as we read
Read back as we gobble the words up.
Allowing the poem to represent
A recognizable landscape
Sprouting green up or letting green
With all its weight of love hang
To gravity's sweet affection,
Arse-versa it is the same object,
Even although the last word seems
To have sung first, or the breakfast lark
Sings up from the bottom of the sea.

11

The poem is not a string of knots
Tied for a meaning of another time
And country, unreadable, found
By chance. The poem is not a henge
Or Easter Island emerged Longnose
Or a tally used by early unknown
Peoples. The words we breathe and puff
Are our utensils down the dream
Into the manhole. Replace the cover.

[29]

The words are mine. The thoughts are all
Yours as they occur behind
The bat of your vast unseen eyes.
These words are as you see them put
Down on the dead-still page. They have
No ability above their station.
Their station on silence is exact.
What you do with them is nobody's business.

Running across the language lightly
This morning in the hangingover
Whistling light from the window, I
Was tripped and caught into the whole
Formal scheme which Art is.
I had only meant to enjoy
Dallying between the imaginary
And imaginary's opposite
With a thought or two up my sleeve.

Is the word? Yes Yes. But I hear
A sound without words from another
Person I can't see at my elbow.
A sigh to be proud of. You? Me?

Having to construct the silence first
To speak out on I realize
The silence even itself floats

At my ear-side with a character
I have not met before. Hello
Hello I shout but that silence
Floats steady, will not be marked
By an off-hand shout. For some reason
It refuses to be broken now
By what I thought was worth saying.
If I wait a while, if I look out
At the heavy greedy rooks on the wall
It will disperse. Now I construct
A new silence I hope to break.

THE THERMAL STAIR

For the painter Peter Lanyon killed in a gliding
accident 1964

I called today, Peter, and you were away.
I look out over Botallack and over Ding
Dong and Levant and over the jasper sea.

Find me a thermal to speak and soar to you from
Over Lanyon Quoit and the circling stones standing
High on the moor over Gurnard's Head where some

Time three foxglove summers ago, you came.
The days are shortening over Little Parc Owles.
The poet or painter steers his life to maim

Himself somehow for the job. His job is Love
Imagined into words or paint to make
An object that will stand and will not move.

Peter, I called and you were away, speaking
Only through what you made and at your best.
Look, there above Botallack, the buzzard riding

The salt updraught slides off the broken air
And out of sight to quarter a new place.
The Celtic sea, the Methodist sea is there.

> You said once in the Engine
> House below Morvah
> That words make their world
> In the same way as the painter's
> Mark surprises him
> Into seeing new.
> Sit here on the sparstone

In this ruin where
Once the early beam
Engine pounded and broke
The air with industry.

Now the chuck of daws
And the listening sea.

"Shall we go down" you said
"Before the light goes
And stand under the old
Tinworkings around
Morvah and St Just?"
You said "Here is the sea
Made by alfred wallis
Or any poet or painter's
Eye it encountered.
Or is it better made
By all those vesselled men
Sometime it maintained?
We all make it again."

Give me your hand, Peter,
To steady me on the word.

Seventy-two by sixty,
Italy hangs on the wall.
A woman stands with a drink
In some polite place
And looks at SARACINESCO
And turns to mention space.
That one if she could
Would ride Artistically
The thermals you once rode.

Peter, the phallic boys
Begin to wink their lights.

Godrevy and the Wolf
Are calling Opening Time.
We'll take the quickest way
The tin singers made.
Climb here where the hand
Will not grasp on air.
And that dark-suited man
Has set the dominoes out
On the Queen's table.
Peter, we'll sit and drink
And go in the sea's roar
To Labrador with wallis
Or rise on Lanyon's stair.

Uneasy, lovable man, give me your painting
Hand to steady me taking the word-road home.
Lanyon, why is it you're earlier away?
Remember me wherever you listen from.
Lanyon, dingdong dingdong from carn to carn.
It seems tonight all Closing bells are tolling
Across the Duchy shire wherever I turn.

THE BEAST IN THE SPACE

Shut up. Shut up. There's nobody here.
If you think you hear somebody knocking
On the other side of the words, pay
No attention. It will be only
The great creature that thumps its tail
On silence on the other side.
If you do not even hear that
I'll give the beast a quick skelp
And through Art you'll hear it yelp.

The beast that lives on silence takes
Its bite out of either side.
It pads and sniffs between us. Now
It comes and laps my meaning up.
Call it over. Call it across
This curious necessary space.
Get off, you terrible inhabiter
Of silence. I'll not have it. Get
Away to whoever it is will have you.

He's gone and if he's gone to you
That's fair enough. For on this side
Of the words it's late. The heavy moth
Bangs on the pane. The whole house
Is sleeping and I remember
I am not here, only the space
I sent the terrible beast across.
Watch. He bites. Listen gently
To any song he snorts or growls
And give him food. He means neither
Well or ill towards you. Above
All, shut up. Give him your love.

THE FOUND PICTURE

Flame and the garden we are together
In it using our secret time up.
We are together in this picture.

It is of the Early Italian School
And not great, a landscape
Maybe illustrating a fable.

We are those two figures barely
Discernible in the pool under
The umbra of the foreground tree.

Or that is how I see it. Nothing
Will move. This is a holy picture
Under its varnish darkening.

2

The Tree of Life unwraps its leaves
And makes its fruit like lightning.
Beyond the river the olive groves.

Beyond the olives musical sounds
Are heard. It is the old, authentic
Angels weeping out of bounds.

3

Observe how the two creatures turn
Slowly toward each other each
In the bare buff and yearning in

Their wordless place. The light years
Have over-varnished them to keep
Them still in their classic secrets.

I slant the canvas. Now look in
To where under the cracking black,
A third creature hides by the spring.

The painted face is faded with light
And the couple are aware of him.
They turn their tufts out of his sight

In this picture's language not
Wanting to be discovered. He
Is not a bad man or a caught

Tom peeping out of his true time.
He is a god making a funny
Face across the world's garden.

See they are fixed they cannot move
Within the landscape of our eyes.
What shall we say out of love

Turning toward each other to hide
In somewhere the breaking garden?
What shall we say to the hiding god?

LINES ON ROGER HILTON'S WATCH

Which I was given because
I loved him and we had
Terrible times together.

O tarnished ticking time
Piece with your bent hand,
You must be used to being
Looked at suddenly
In the middle of the night
When he switched the light on
Beside his bed. I hope
You told him the best time
When he lifted you up
To meet the Hilton gaze.

I lift you up from the mantel
Piece here in my house
Wearing your verdigris.
At least I keep you wound
And put my ear to you
To hear Botallack tick.

You realise your master
Has relinquished you
And gone to lie under
The ground at St Just.

Tell me the time. The time
Is Botallack o'clock.
This is the dead of night.

He switches the light on
To find a cigarette

And pours himself a Teachers.
He picks me up and holds me
Near his lonely face
To see my hands. He thinks
He is not being watched.

The images of his dream
Are still about his face
As he spits and tries not
To remember where he was.

I am only a watch
And pray time hastes away.
I think I am running down.
Watch, it is time I wound
You up again. I am
Very much not your dear
Last master but we had
Terrible times together.

DEAR BRYAN WYNTER

1

This is only a note
To say how sorry I am
You died. You will realise
What a position it puts
Me in. I couldn't really
Have died for you if so
I were inclined. The carn
Foxglove here on the wall
Outside your first house
Leans with me standing
In the Zennor wind.

Anyhow how are things?
Are you still somewhere
With your long legs
And twitching smile under
Your blue hat walking
Across a place? Or am
I greedy to make you up
Again out of memory?
Are you there at all?
I would like to think
You were all right
And not worried about
Monica and the children
And not unhappy or bored.

Speaking to you and not
Knowing if you are there

Is not too difficult.
My words are used to that.
Do you want anything?
Where shall I send something?
Rice-wine, meanders, paintings
By your contemporaries?
Or shall I send a kind
Of news of no time
Leaning against the wall
Outside your old house.

The house and the whole moor
Is flying in the mist.

3

I am up. I've washed
The front of my face
And here I stand looking
Out over the top
Half of my bedroom window.
There almost as far
As I can see I see
St Buryan's church tower.
An inch to the left, behind
That dark rise of woods,
Is where you used to lurk.

4

This is only a note
To say I am aware
You are not here. I find
It difficult to go
Beside Housman's star

Lit fences without you.
And nobody will laugh
At my jokes like you.

5

Bryan, I would be obliged
If you would scout things out
For me. Although I am not
Just ready to start out.
I am trying to be better,
Which will make you smile
Under your blue hat.

I know I make a symbol
Of the foxglove on the wall.
It is because it knows you.

BALDY BANE

Shrill the fife, kettle the drum,
   My Queens my Sluts my Beauties
Show me your rich attention
   Among the shower of empties.
And quiet be as it was once
   It fell on a night late
The muse has felled me in this bed
   That in the wall is set.
Lie over to me from the wall or else
   Get up and clean the grate.

On such a night as this behind
   McKellar's Tanworks' wall
It seems I put my hand in hers
   As we played at the ball.
So began a folly that
   I hope will linger late,
Though I am of the kitchen bed
   And of the flannel sheet.
Lie over to me from the wall or else
   Get up and clean the grate.

Now pay her no attention now,
   Nor that we keep our bed.
It is yon hoodie on the gate
   Would speak me to the dead.
And though I am embedded here
   The creature to forget
I ask you one and all to come.
   Let us communicate.
Lie over to me from the wall or else
   Get up and clean the grate.

Make yourself at home here.
  My words you move within.
I made them all by hand for you
  To use as your own.
Yet I'll not have it said that they
  Leave my intention out,
Else I, an old man, I will up
  And at that yella-yite.
Lie over to me from the wall or else
  Get up and clean the grate.

You're free to jig your fiddle or let
  It dally on the bow.
Who's he that bums his chat there,
  Drunk as a wheelbarrow?
Hey, you who visit an old man
  That a young wife has got,
Mind your brain on the beam there
  And watch the lentil pot.
Lie over to me from the wall or else
  Get up and clean the grate.

Now pay her no attention.
  I am the big bowbender.
These words shall lie the way I want
  Or she'll blacklead the fender.
No shallop she, her length and depth
  Is Clyde and clinker built.
When I have that one shafted I
  Allow my best to out.
Lie over to me from the wall or else
  Get up and clean the grate.

Full as a whelk, full as a whelk
  And sad when all is done.
The children cry me Baldy Bane
  And the great catches are gone.

But do you know my mother's tune,
    For it is very sweet?
I split my thumb upon the barb
    The last time I heard it.
Lie over to me from the wall or else
    Get up and clean the grate.

Squeeze the box upon the tune
    They call Kate Dalrymple O.
Cock your ears upon it and
    To cock your legs is simple O.
Full as a whelk, full as a whelk
    And all my hooks to bait.
Is that the nightshift knocking off?
    I hear men in the street.
Lie over to me from the wall or else
    Get up and clean the grate.

Move to me as you birl, Meg.
    Your mother was a great whore.
I have not seen such pas de bas
    Since up in Kirriemuir.
I waded in your shallows once,
    Now drink up to that.
It makes the blood go up and down
    And lifts the sneck a bit.
Lie over to me from the wall or else
    Get up and clean the grate.

Through the word and through the word,
    And all is sad and done,
Who are you that these words
    Make this fall upon?
Fair's fair, upon my word,
    And that you shall admit,
Or I will blow your face in glass
    And then I'll shatter it.

Lie over to me from the wall or else
    Get up and clean the grate.

If there's a joke between us
    Let it lie where it fell.
The exact word escapes me
    And that's just as well.
I always have the tune by ear.
    You are an afterthought.
But when the joke and the grief strike
    Your heart beats on the note.
Lie over to me from the wall or else
    Get up and clean the grate.

Full as a whelk, full as a whelk
    My brain is blanketstitched.
It is the drink has floored us
    And Meg lies unlatched.
Lie over to me, my own muse.
    The bed is our estate.
Here's a drink to caulk your seams
    Against the birling spate.
Lie over to me from the wall or else
    Get up and clean the grate.

Now pay her no attention, you.
    Your gears do not engage.
By and large it's meet you should
    Keep to your gelded cage.
My ooze, my merry-making muse,
    You're nothing to look at.
But prow is proud and rudder rude
    Is the long and short of that.
Lie over to me from the wall or else
    Get up and clean the grate.

Think of a word and double it.
　　Admit my metaphor.
But leave the muscle in the verse,
　　It is the Skerry Vore.
Can you wash a sailor's shirt
　　And can you wash it white?
O can you wash a sailor's shirt
　　The whitest in the fleet?
Lie over to me from the wall or else
　　Get up and clean the grate.

Full as a whelk and ending,
　　Surprise me to my lot.
The glint of the great catches
　　Shall not again be caught.
But the window is catching
　　The slow mend of light.
Who crossed these words before me
　　Crossed my meaning out.
Lie over to me from the wall or else
　　Get up and clean the grate.

Cry me Baldy Bane but cry
　　The hoodie off the gate,
And before you turn away
　　Turn to her last estate.
She lies to fell me on the field
　　Of silence I wrote.
By whose endeavour do we fare?
　　By the word in her throat.
Lie over to me from the wall or else
　　Get up and clean the grate.

She lies to fell me on the field
　　That is between us here.
I have but to lift the sneck
　　With a few words more.

Take kindly to Baldy Bane, then
  And go your ways about.
Tell it in the Causewayside
  And in Cartsburn Street,
Lie over to me from the wall or else
  Get up and clean the grate.

Love me near, love me far.
  Lie over from the wall.
You have had the best of me
  Since we played at the ball.
I cross the Fingal of my stride
  With you at beauty heat.
And I burn my words behind me.
  Silence is shouted out.
Lie over to me from the wall or else
  Get up and clean the grate.

MEN SIGN THE SEA

Men sign the sea.
One warbreath more sucked round the roaring veins
Keeping the heart in ark then down loud mountains
After his cry.

This that the sea
Moves through moves over sea-tongued the whole waters
Woven over their breath. So can the floating fires
Blow down on any.

This deep time, scaling broadside the cannoning sea,
Tilting, cast rigged among galloping iron vesselwork,
Snapped wirerope, spitting oil, steam screamed out jets,
Bomb drunkard hero herded by the hammerheaded elements,
Loud raftered foamfloored house, a waved scorched hand
Over final upheaval and the decked combers.
The filling limpet shell's slow gyre round the drowned.
The cairns of foam stand up. The signed sea flowers.

The love-signed sea
Weeded with words and branched with human ores
Lights up. An arm waves off the land. Thunderous
Time mines the sea.

Men sign the sea,
Maintained on memory's emerald over the drowned.
This that the sea moves through drives through the land
Twin to their cry.

THE NIGHTFISHING

Very gently struck
The quay night bell.

Now within the dead
Of night and the dead
Of my life I hear
My name called from far out.
I'm come to this place
(Come to this place)
Which I'll not pass
Though one shall pass
Wearing seemingly
This look I move as.
This staring second
Breaks my home away
Through always every
Night through every whisper
From the first that once
Named me to the bone.
Yet this place finds me
And forms itself again.
This present place found me.
Owls from on the land.
Gulls cry from the water.
And that wind honing
The roof-ridge is out of
Nine hours west on the main
Ground with likely a full
Gale unwinding it.

Gently the quay bell
Strikes the held air.

Strikes the held air like
Opening a door
So that all the dead
Brought to harmony
Speak out on silence.

I bent to the lamp. I cupped
My hand to the glass chimney.
Yet it was a stranger's breath
From out of my mouth that
Shed the light. I turned out
Into the salt dark
And turned my collar up.

And now again almost
Blindfold with the bright
Hemisphere unprised
Ancient overhead,
I am befriended by
This sea which utters me.

The hull slewed out through
The lucky turn and trembled
Under way then. The twin
Screws spun sweetly alive
Spinning position away.

Far out faintly calls
The continual sea.

Now within the dead
Of night and the dead
Of all my life I go.
I'm one ahead of them
Turned in below.
I'm borne, in their eyes,
Through the staring world.

The present opens its arms.

To work at waking. Yet who wakes?
Dream gives awake its look. My death
Already has me clad anew.
We'll move off in this changing grace.
The moon keels and the harbour oil
Looks at the sky through seven colours.

When I fell down into this place
My father drew his whole day's pay,
My mother lay in a set-in bed,
The midwife threw my bundle away.

Here we dress up in a new grave,
The fish-boots with their herring scales
Inlaid as silver of a good week,
The jersey knitted close as nerves
Of the ground under the high bracken.
My eyes let light in on this dark.

When I fell from the hot to the cold
My father drew his whole day's pay,
My mother lay in a set-in bed,
The midwife threw my bundle away.

3

I, in Time's grace, the grace of change, sail surely
Moved off the land and the skilled keel sails
The darkness burning under where I go.
Landvoices and the lights ebb away
Raising the night round us. Unwinding whitely,
My changing motive pays me slowly out.
The sea sails in. The quay opens wide its arms
And waves us loose.

So I would have it, waved from home to out
After that, the continual other offer,
Intellect sung in a garment of innocence.
Here, formal and struck into a dead stillness,
The voyage sails you no more than your own.
And on its wrought epitaph fathers itself
The sea as metaphor of the sea. The boat
Rides in its fires.

And nursed now out on movement as we go,
Running white from the bow, the long keel sheathed
In departure leaving the sucked and slackening water
As mingled in memory; night rises stooped high over
Us as our boat keeps its nets and men and
Engraves its wake. Our bow heaves hung on a likely
Bearing for fish. The Mor Light flashes astern
Dead on its second.

Across our moving local of light the gulls
Go in a wailing slant. I watch, merged
In this and in a like event, as the boat
Takes the mild swell, and each event speaks through.
They speak me thoroughly to my faintest breath.
And for what sake? Each word is but a longing
Set out to break from a difficult home. Yet in
Its meaning I am.

The weather's come round. For us it's better broken.
Changed and shifted above us, the sky is broken
Now into a few light patches brightly ground
With its rough smithers and those swells lengthening
Easy on us, outride us in a slow follow
From stern to stem. The keel in its amorous furrow
Goes through each word. He drowns, who but ill
Resembled me.

In those words through which I move, leaving a cry
Formed in exact degree and set dead at
The mingling flood, I am put forward on to
Live water, clad in oil, burnt by salt
To life. Here, braced, announced on to the slow
Heaving seaboards, almost I am now too
Lulled. And my watch is blear. The early grey
Air is blowing.

It is that first pallor there, broken, running
Back on the sheared water. Now the chill wind
Comes off the shore sharp to find its old mark
Between the shoulderblades. My eyes read in
The fixed and flying signs wound in the light
Which all shall soon lie wound in as it slowly
Approaches rising to break wide up over the
Brow of the sea.

My need reads in light more specially gendered and
Ambitioned by all eyes that wide have been
Me once. The cross-tree light, yellowing now,
Swings clean across Orion. And waned and very
Gently the old signs tilt and somersault
Towards their home. The undertow, come hard round,
Now leans the tiller strongly jammed over
On my hip-bone.

It is us at last sailed into the chance
Of a good take. For there is the water gone
Lit black and wrought like iron into the look
That's right for herring. We dropped to the single motor.
The uneasy and roused gulls slid across us with
Swelled throats screeching. Our eyes sharpened what
Place we made through them. Now almost the light
To shoot the nets,

And keep a slow headway. One last check
To the gear. Our mended newtanned nets, all ropes
Loose and unkinked, tethers and springropes fast,
The tethers generous with floats to ride high,
And the big white bladder floats at hand to heave.
The bow wakes hardly a spark at the black hull.
The night and day both change their flesh about
In merging levels.

No more than merely leaning on the sea
We move. We move on this near-stillness enough
To keep the rudder live and gripped in the keel-wash.
We're well hinted herring plenty for the taking,
About as certain as all those signs falling
Through their appearance. Gulls settle lightly forward
Then scare off wailing as the sea-dusk lessens
Over our stern.

Yes, we're right set, see, see them go down, the best
Fishmarks, the gannets. They wheel high for a moment
Then heel, slip off the bearing air to plummet
Into the schooling sea. It's right for shooting,
Fish breaking the oiled water, the sea still
Holding its fires. Right, easy ahead, we'll run
Them straight out lined to the west. Now they go over,
White float and rope

And the net fed out in arm-lengths over the side.
So we shoot out the slowly diving nets
Like sowing grain. There they drag back their drifting
Weight out astern, a good half-mile of corks
And bladders. The last net's gone and we make fast
And cut the motor. The corks in a gentle wake,
Over curtains of water, tether us stopped, lapped
At far last still.

It is us no more moving, only the mere
Maintaining levels as they mingle together.
Now round the boat, drifting its drowning curtains
A grey of light begins. These words take place.
The petrel dips at the water-fats. And quietly
The stillness makes its way to its ultimate home.
The bilges slap. Gulls wail and settle.
It is us still.

At last it's all so still. We hull to the nets,
And rest back with our shoulders slacked pleasantly.
And I am illusioned out of this flood as
Separate and stopped to trace all grace arriving.
This grace, this movement bled into this place,
Locks the boat still in the grey of the seized sea.
The illuminations of innocence embrace.
What measures gently

Cross in the air to us to fix us so still
In this still brightness by knowledge of
The quick proportions of our intricacies?
What sudden perfection is this the measurement of?
And speaks us thoroughly to the bone and has
The iron sea engraved to our faintest breath,
The spray fretted and fixed at a high temper,
A script of light.

So I have been called by my name and
It was not sound. It is me named upon
The space which I continually move across
Bearing between my courage and my lack
The constant I bleed on. And, put to stillness,
Fixed in this metal and its cutting salts,
It is this instant to exact degree,
And for whose sake?

It is this instant written dead. This instant,
Bounded by its own grace and all Time's grace,
Masters me into its measurement so that
My ghostly constant is articulated.
Then suddenly like struck rock all points unfix.
The whole east breaks and leans at last to us,
Ancient overhead. Yet not a break of light
But mingles into

The whole memory of light, and will not cease
Contributing its exiled quality.
The great morning moves from its equivalent
Still where it lies struck in expressed proportion.
The streaming morning in its tensile light
Leans to us and looks over on the sea.
It's time to haul. The air stirs its faint pressures,
A slat of wind.

We are at the hauling then hoping for it
The hard slow haul of a net white with herring
Meshed hard. I haul, using the boat's cross-heave
We've started, holding fast as we rock back,
Taking slack as we go to. The day rises brighter
Over us and the gulls rise in a wailing scare
From the nearest net-floats. And the unfolding water
Mingles its dead.

Now better white I can say what's better sighted,
The white net flashing under the watched water,
The near net dragging back with the full belly
Of a good take certain, so drifted easy
Slow down on us or us hauled up upon it
Curved in a garment down to thicker fathoms.
The hauling nets come in sawing the gunwale
With herring scales.

The air bunches to a wind and roused sea-cries.
The weather moves and stoops high over us and
There the forked tern, where my look's whetted on
　　　distance,
Quarters its hunting sea. I haul slowly
Inboard the drowning flood as into memory,
Braced at the breathside in my net of nerves.
We haul and drift them home. The winds slowly
Turn round on us and

Gather towards us with dragging weights of water
Sleekly swelling across the humming sea
And gather heavier. We haul and hold and haul
Well the bright chirpers home, so drifted whitely
All a blinding garment out of the grey water.
And, hauling hard in the drag, the nets come in,
The headrope a sore pull and feeding its brine
Into our hacked hands.

Over the gunwale over into our deep lap
The herring come in, staring from their scales,
Fruitful as our deserts would have it out of
The deep and shifting seams of water. We haul
Against time fallen ill over the gathering
Rush of the sea together. The calms dive down.
The strident kingforked airs roar in their shell.
We haul the last

Net home and the last tether off the gathering
Run of the started sea. And then was the first
Hand at last lifted getting us swung against
Into the homing quarter, running that white grace
That sails me surely ever away from home.
And we hold into it as it moves down on
Us running white on the hull heeled to light.
Our bow heads home

Into the running blackbacks soaring us loud
High up in open arms of the towering sea.
The steep bow heaves, hung on these words, towards
What words your lonely breath blows out to meet it.
It is the skilled keel itself knowing its own
Fathoms it further moves through, with us there
Kept in its common timbers, yet each of us
Unwound upon

By a lonely behaviour of the all common ocean.
I cried headlong from my dead. The long rollers,
Quick on the crests and shirred with fine foam,
Surge down then sledge their green tons weighing dead
Down on the shuddered deck-boards. And shook off
All that white arrival upon us back to falter
Into the waking spoil and to be lost in
The mingling world.

So we were started back over that sea we
Had worked widely all fish-seasons and over
Its shifting grounds, yet now risen up into
Such humours, I felt like a farmer tricked to sea.
For it sailed sore against us. It grew up
To black banks that crossed us. It stooped, beaked.
Its brine burnt us. I was chosen and given.
It rose as risen

Treachery becomes myself, to clip me amorously
Off from all common breath. Those fires burned
Sprigs of the foam and branching tines of water.
It rose so white, soaring slowly, up
On us, then broke, down on us. It became a mull
Against our going and unfastened under us and
Curdled from the stern. It shipped us at each blow.
The brute weight

Of the living sea wrought us, yet the boat sleeked lean
Into it, upheld by the whole sea-brunt heaved,
And hung on the swivelling tops. The tiller raised
The siding tide to wrench us and took a good
Ready hand to hold it. Yet we made a seaway
And minded all the gear was fast, and took
Our spell at steering. And we went keeled over
The streaming sea.

See how, like an early self, it's loath to leave
And stares from the scuppers as it swirls away
To be clenched up. What a great width stretches
Farsighted away fighting in its white straits
On either bow, but bears up our boat on all
Its plaiting strands. This wedge driven in
To the twisting water, we rode. The bow shores
The long rollers.

The keel climbs and, with screws spinning out of their bite,
We drive down into the roar of the great doorways,
Each time almost to overstay, but start
Up into again the yelling gale and hailing
Shot of the spray. Yet we should have land
Soon marking us out of this thick distance and
How far we're in. Who is that poor sea-scholar,
Braced in his hero,

Lost in his book of storms there? It is myself.
So he who died is announced. This mingling element
Gives up myself. Words travel from what they once
Passed silence with. Here, in this intricate death,
He goes as fixed on silence as ever he'll be.
Leave him, nor cup a hand to shout him out
Of that, his home. Or, if you would, O surely
There is no word,

There is not any to go over that.
It is now as always this difficult air
We look towards each other through. And is there
Some singing look or word or gesture of grace
Or naked wide regard from the encountered face,
Goes ever true through the difficult air?
Each word speaks its own speaker to his death.
And we saw land

At last marked on the tenting mist and we could
Just make out the ridge running from the north
To the Black Rosses, and even mark the dark hint
Of Skeer well starboard. Now inside the bight
The sea was loosening and the screws spun steadier
Beneath us. We still shipped the blown water but
It broke white, not green weight caved in on us.
In out of all

That forming and breaking sea we came on the long
Swell close at last inshore with the day grey
With mewing distances and mist. The rocks rose
Waving their lazy friendly weed. We came in
Moving now by the world's side. And O the land lay
Just as we knew it well all along that shore
Akin to us with each of its dear seamarks. And lay
Like a mother.

We came in, riding steady in the bay water,
A sailing pillar of gulls, past the cockle strand.
And springing teal came out off the long sand. We
Moved under the soaring land sheathed in fair water
In that time's morning grace. I uttered that place
And left each word I was. The quay-heads lift up
To pass us in. These sea-worked measures end now.
And this element

Ends as we move off from its formal instant.
Now he who takes my place continually anew
Speaks me thoroughly perished into another.
And the quay opened its arms. I heard the sea
Close on him gently swinging on oiled hinges.
Moored here, we cut the motor quiet. He that
I'm not lies down. Men shout. Words break. I am
My fruitful share.

4

Only leaned at rest
Where my home is cast
Cannonwise on silence
And the serving distance.

O my love, keep the day
Leaned at rest, leaned at rest.

Only breathed at ease
In that loneliness
Bragged into a voyage
On the maintaining image.

O my love, there we lay
Loved alone, loved alone.

Only graced in my
Changing madman who
Sings but has no time
To divine my room.

O my love, keep the day
Leaned at rest, leaned at rest.

What one place remains
Home as darkness quickens?

5

So this is the place. This
Is the place fastened still with movement,
Movement as calligraphic and formal as
A music burned on copper.

At this place
The eye reads forward as the memory reads back.
At this last word all words change.
All words change in acknowledgement of the last.
Here is their mingling element.
This is myself (who but ill resembles me).
He befriended so many
Disguises to wander in on as many roads
As cross on a ball of wool.
What a stranger he's brought to pass
Who sits here in his place.
What a man arrived breathless
With a look or word to a few
Before he's off again.

Here is this place no more
Certain though the steep streets
And High Street form again and the sea
Swing shut on hinges and the doors all open wide.

6

As leaned at rest in lamplight with
The offered moth and heard breath
By grace of change serving my birth,

And as at hushed called by the owl,
With my chair up to my salt-scrubbed table,
While my endured walls kept me still,

I leaned and with a kind word gently
Struck the held air like a doorway
Bled open to meet another's eye.

Lie down, my recent madman, hardly
Drawn into breath than shed to memory,
For there you'll labour less lonely.

Lie down and serve. Your death is past.
There the fishing ground is richest.
There contribute your sleight of cast.

The rigged ship in its walls of glass
Still further forms its perfect seas
Locked in its past transparences.

You're come among somewhere the early
Children at play who govern my way
And shed each tear which burns my eye.

Thus, shed into the industrious grave
Ever of my life, you serve the love
Whose motive we are energies of.

So quietly my words upon the air
Awoke their harmonies for ever
Contending within the ear they alter.

And as the lamp burned back the silence
And the walls caved to a clear lens,
The room again became my distance.

I sat rested at the grave's table
Saying his epitaph who shall
Be after me to shout farewell.

Far out, faintly rocked,
Struck the sea bell.

Home becomes this place,
A bitter night, ill
To labour at dead of.
Within all the dead of
All my life I hear
My name spoken out
On the break of the surf.
I, in Time's grace,
The grace of change, am
Cast into memory.
What a restless grace
To trace stillness on.

Now this place about me
Wakes the night's twin shafts
And sheds the quay slowly.
Very gently the keel
Walks its waters again.
The sea awakes its fires.
White water stares in
From the harbour-mouth.
And we run through well
Held off the black land
Out into the waving
Nerves of the open sea.

My dead in the crew
Have mixed all qualities
That I have been and,
Though ghosted behind
My sides spurred by the spray,

Endure by a further gaze
Pearled behind my eyes.
Far out faintly calls
The mingling sea.

Now again blindfold
With the hemisphere
Unprised and bright
Ancient overhead,

This present place is
Become made into
A breathless still place
Unrolled on a scroll
And turned to face this light.

So I spoke and died.
So within the dead
Of night and the dead
Of all my life those
Words died and awoke.

GREENOCK AT NIGHT I FIND YOU

1

As for you loud Greenock long ropeworking
Hide and seeking rivetting town of my child
Hood, I know we think of us often mostly
At night. Have you ever desired me back
Into the set-in bed at the top of the land
In One Hope Street? I am myself lying
Half-asleep hearing the rivetting yards
And smelling the bone-works with no home
Work done for Cartsburn School in the morning.

At night. And here I am descending and
The welding lights in the shipyards flower blue
Under my hopeless eyelids as I lie
Sleeping conditioned to hide from happy.

2

So what did I do? I walked from Hope Street
Down Lyndoch Street between the night's words
To Cartsburn Street and got to the Cartsburn Vaults
With half an hour to go. See, I am back.

3

See, I am back. My father turned and I saw
He had the stick he cut in Sheelhill Glen.
Brigit was there and Hugh and double-breasted
Sam and Malcolm Mooney and Alastair Graham.
They all were there in the Cartsburn Vaults shining
To meet me but I was only remembered.

TO ALEXANDER GRAHAM

Lying asleep walking
Last night I met my father
Who seemed pleased to see me.
He wanted to speak. I saw
His mouth saying something
But the dream had no sound.

We were surrounded by
Laid-up paddle steamers
In The Old Quay in Greenock.
I smelt the tar and the ropes.

It seemed that I was standing
Beside the big iron cannon
The tugs used to tie up to
When I was a boy. I turned
To see Dad standing just
Across the causeway under
That one lamp they keep on.

He recognised me immediately.
I could see that. He was
The handsome, same age
With his good brows as when
He would take me on Sundays
Saying we'll go for a walk.

Dad, what am I doing here?
What is it I am doing now?
Are you proud of me?
Going away, I knew
You wanted to tell me something.

You stopped and almost turned back
To say something. My father,
I try to be the best
In you you give me always.

Lying asleep turning
Round in the quay-lit dark
It was my father standing
As real as life. I smelt
The quay's tar and the ropes.

I think he wanted to speak.
But the dream had no sound.
I think I must have loved him.

JOHANN JOACHIM QUANTZ'S
FIRST LESSON

So that each person may quickly find that
Which particularly concerns him, certain metaphors
Convenient to us within the compass of this
Lesson are to be allowed. It is best I sit
Here where I am to speak on the other side
Of language. You, of course, in your own time
And incident (I speak in the small hours.)
Will listen from your side. I am very pleased
We have sought us out. No doubt you have read
My Flute Book. Come. The Guild clock's iron men
Are striking out their few deserted hours
And here from my high window Brueghel's winter
Locks the canal below. I blow my fingers.

THE NARRATOR

I am the hawk-heart braced in the epic's hero
Hollow and lit in a single follyless zone
Twinned with a dawn and a dark.
Graceless in gardens I hear my unvisited care
Squawk back at the sculptured cuckoo's nursery rhyme
Chimed in the dandelion tower.
Eyelashed and petald alone in the shepherd season
I walk heaved high from the earth confessing the voice
That runs ever over the hour
Confessing the death without space for the laying of dead
The rudder and rocket stem and the murder swerve
At the tender right-wrong heart.

The hiccuping hero the narrator lindenward
Reels at the waltz with diaphanous water fronds
Telling his ribbed in vanity.
I worship a skylift of Narnain blaeberry globed
Priestlike sealed in a tensile sac in a nerve
In the vein-geared bubble of vision.
While whisper the tethered anemones under the grave
And the narrative sprouts from the bone-sweet skull
Telling a blossom to its bulb
And spins in a hollow of sound in the emerald dome
Tinctured vermilion and told in the glacier heart
That trades the unmapped spell along the blood.

The raven at larch time dwarfed in the calyxed chronicle
In my head's helmet weathers no wheeling sky.
The banished bird spins no horizon.
Yet my eye webs the word. History in a bowl
Spreads out a firth for ptarmigan and the pedlar's moth
And anarchy within a cage.

Who knows the rose or quotes her holy somersaults
Preached from a dangled spinner on a maypole thread.
What summer eyes perched deep within a dream
Could bring the god the child and the rose to speak.
What tongue like a stamen stemmed on a kiss or a grave
Is yet enchanted into form.

EXPLANATION OF A MAP

Near farms and property of bright night-time
By mileaway dogbark how there is means to say
What unseen bargain makes heavier where I walk
The meanwhile word here of this neighbourhood.
Mileaway for answer tilling the fertile sky
Direction's breakdown assembles my own heaven
Builds up, breaks the dead quarter into miles
With towering tongue of each discovering hour.
Some loud means in the dark for my sake tells
My journey manned and sailed but none so man,
Bullhorned, treehorned from the heads of huntsmen.

As man sets out under his roof of lanterns
Joisted hawthorn and a thousand fabled bonfires
I take the starry whiphand quick with means
Blood, maid, and man, as they set out to be
Fruitful in each house and fulfil all seas.
By side of trespass under this same roof
What further tests knock under lock and keep,
Catapult famously as I have worn my fires
Curled in the scoop of fear? The shell to weep
Back simple seas, eyewitness to hell and heaven,
Is now for man's sake manfully the measuring watchman.

Good stars above you, night pedestrian.
How do you pleasure and approach the prize?
By side of canted sin set in my zones
I strip the crimes of west from my flat palm.
As man breaks flight alone in a blue disguise
Love scarlet on its axis of gone days
Tilts a new measure for pain in a crush of pleasure.
I am parliament in a roaring way. My word
Knows mister and missus, measure and live feature,

So fume and jet of the floor and all its towns
Wording the world awake and all its suns.

Under the bright ventriloquist the quiet
Animal raises and knocks the years to war.
Under the process of the flooding sky
Deeps in the desert know no rising up.
Near gates and fences astronomy's possessions
On whinny fields creep through the precious pools.
I cast, before peace grips my world's stoked womb,
High my bled ground. O over me the cambered
Wave, motive to all to tell the untold room,
Tells fable and fire. My eyes drown where they lie.
Grief with a silent oar circles to say.

HERE NEXT THE CHAIR I WAS
WHEN WINTER WENT

Here next the chair I was when winter went
Down looking for distant bothies of love
And met birch-bright and by the blows of March
The farm bolder under and the din of burning.

I was what the whinfire works on towns
An orator from hill to kitchen dances.
In booths below bridges that spanned the crowds
Tinkers tricked glasses on lips and saw my eyes.

Like making a hut of fingers cupped for tears
Love burned my bush that was my burning mother.
The hoodiecrow in smoke in a wobbling wind
If a look is told for fortune saw my death.

So still going out in the morning of ash and air
My shovel swings. My tongue is a sick device.
Fear evening my boot says. The chair sees iceward
In the bitter hour so visible to death.

THE LYING DEAR

At entrance cried out but not
For me (Should I have needed it?)
Her bitching eyes under
My pressing down shoulder
Looked up to meet the face
In cracks on the flaking ceiling

Descending. The map of damp
Behind me, up, formed
Itself to catch the look
Under the closed (now)
Lids of my lying dear.

Under my pinning arm
I suddenly saw between
The acting flutters, a look
Catch on some image not me.

With a hand across her eyes
I changed my weight of all
Knowledge of her before.
And like a belly sledge
I steered us on the run
Mounting the curves to almost
The high verge. Her breath
Flew out like smoke. Her beauty
Twisted into another
Beauty and we went down
Into the little village
Of a new language.

DEAR WHO I MEAN

Dear who I mean but more
Than because of the lonely stumble
In the spiked bramble after
The wrecked dragon caught
In the five high singing wires
Its tail twisting the wind
Into visibility, I turn
To where is it you lodge
Now at the other end
Of this letter let out
On the end of its fine string
Across your silent airts.

There is more to it than just
A boy losing his kite
On a young day. My flying
Stem and cooper's hoop
And printed paper bucks
And stalls then leaves the air
I thought I had made it for.

When the word or the word's name
Flies out before us in winter
Beware of the cunning god
Slinking across the tense
Fields ready to pretend
To carry in spittled jaws
The crashed message, this letter
Between us. With two fingers
I give one whistle along
The frozen black sticks
To bring him to heel. He knows
He is better over a distance.

And now when the wind falls
Disentangle the string. Kill
The creature if so you move.
Use the material of
Its artifice. You might even
Reassemble for your own sake
A dragon to live your life with.

But the quick brown pouncing god
Magnifies towards us.
He crunches it up like a bird
And does not leave one word.

LETTER IV

Night winked and endeared
Itself to language. Huge
Over the dark verge sauntered
Half the moon. Then all
Its shoal attending stared
Down on the calm and mewing
Firth and in a bright
Breath that night became
You in these words fondly
Through me. Even becomes
Us now. And casts me always
Through who I thought I was.
May Love not cast us out.

Know me by the voice
That speaks outside my choice
And speaks our double breath
Into this formal death.

My dear, here and happy
We are cast off away
Swanning through the slow
Shallows and shearing into
The first heave of the deep
Sea's lusty founds.
And out. Lie here happy
Here on this bed of nets.
Loosen the blouse of night.
It seems no time since we
Lay down to let Love pass.
Past? For almost I stoop
Backward to pick Love up,
From where? My dear, all

You've had of me is always
Here. Lean here. Listen.
Though it is always going.
Nor does it say even
A part, but something else.
Time lowers it into bookmould
Filled with words that lied
To where they came from and
To where they went. Yet, lean
On your elbow here. Listen.

What a great way. So bright.
O the sea is meadowsweet.
That voice talking? It's from
Some family famous for
The sea. There's drink in it.
Where did he drown from, taken
By the sea's barbaric hooks?
Yet lie here, love. Listen
To that voice on the swell
(Old rogue with a skilful keel).
It is that voice which hears
The dog whelk's whimper
And the cockle's call come up
From the deep beds under
Those breaking prisms of water.
And hears old Mooney call Time
Bogtongued like doomsday over
The bar and hears Mooney's
Hanging lamp lapping
The sweet oil from its bowl.

And each word, "this" and "this"
Is that night and your breath
Dying on mine moved out
On always the sea moving

Neither its help nor comfort
Between us. Be held a while.

Old Calum's there. Listen.
This is his song he says,
To pass the time at the tiller.
He's sad drunk. Let him be.
He'll not see, that poor
Harper, bat-blind, stone-daft
(That cough was aconite).
Let him go on. His harp's
Some strung breastbone but sweet.
It's often enough their habit,
The old and answered not.

Then what a fine upstander
I was for the cause of Love.
And what a fine woman's
Man I went sauntering as.

I could sing a tear out of
The drunk or sober or deaf.
My love would lie pleasanter
Than ever she lay before.

Now she who younger lay
Lies lost in the husk of night.
My far my vanished dears
All in your bowers.

Fondly from a beyond
His song moved to my hand
And moves as you move now.
Yet here's the long heave
To move us through. Say
After me here. "Unto
My person to be peer".

And all holds us in the hull
That slides between the waving
Gates and the bow drives
Headlong through the salt
Thicket of the maiden sea.

And shall for Christsake always
Bleed down that streaming door.

YOURS TRULY

In reply to your last letter
Which came in too confused
For words saying "Listen.
And silence even has turned
Away. Listen." Dear Pen
Pal in the distance, beyond
My means, why do you bring
Your face down so near
To affront me here again
With a new expression out
Of not indifferent eyes?
I know you well alas
From where I sit behind
The Art barrier of ice.

Did you hear me call you across
The dead centre of the night?

Where is your pride I said
To myself calling myself
By my name even pronouncing
It freshly I thought but blushed
At the lonely idea.
I saw myself wearing
A clumping taliped
Disguise I was too shy
To take an answer from.

Am I too loud? I hear
Members of the house stirring
Not able to keep asleep
Not able to keep awake
Nor to be satisfactorily

Between. O by the way
I thought I saw you standing
Older losing yourself in
The changed Mooney's mirrors
Of what is left of Ireland.

LANGUAGE AH NOW YOU HAVE ME

Language ah now you have me. Night-time tongue,
Please speak for me between the social beasts
Which quick assail me. Here I am hiding in
The jungle of mistakes of communication.

I know about jungles. I know about unkempt places
Flying toward me when I am getting ready
To pull myself together and plot the place
To speak from. I am at the jungle face
Which is not easily yours. It is my home
Where pigmies hamstring Jumbo and the pleasure
Monkey is plucked from the tree. How pleased I am
To meet you reading and writing on damp paper
In the rain forest beside the Madron River.

2

Which is my home. The great and small breathers,
Experts of speaking, hang and slowly move
To say something or spring in the steaming air
Down to do the great white hunter for ever.

3

Do not disturb me now. I have to extract
A creature with its eggs between the words.
I have to seize it now, otherwise not only
My vanity will be appalled but my good cat
Will not look at me in the same way.

4

Is not to look. We are the ones hanging
On here and there, the dear word's edge wondering
If we are speaking clearly enough or if
The jungle's acoustics are at fault. Baboon,
My soul, is always ready to relinquish
The safe hold and leap on to nothing at all.
At least I hope so. Language now you have me
Trying to be myself but changed into
The wildebeest pursued or the leo pard
Running at stretch beside the Madron River.

5

Too much. I died. I forgot who I was and sent
My heart back with my bearers. How pleased I am
To find you here beside the Madron River
Wanting to be spoken to. It is my home
Where pigmies hamstring Jumbo and the pleasure
Monkey is plucked from the tree.

I LEAVE THIS AT YOUR EAR

For Nessie Dunsmuir

I leave this at your ear for when you wake,
A creature in its abstract cage asleep.
Your dreams blindfold you by the light they make.

The owl called from the naked-woman tree
As I came down by the Kyle farm to hear
Your house silent by the speaking sea.

I have come late but I have come before
Later with slaked steps from stone to stone
To hope to find you listening for the door.

I stand in the ticking room. My dear, I take
A moth kiss from your breath. The shore gulls cry.
I leave this at your ear for when you wake.

THE NIGHT CITY

Unmet at Euston in a dream
Of London under Turner's steam
Misting the iron gantries, I
Found myself running away
From Scotland into the golden city.

I ran down Gray's Inn Road and ran
Till I was under a black bridge.
This was me at nineteen
Late at night arriving between
The buildings of the City of London.

And then I (O I have fallen down)
Fell in my dream beside the Bank
Of England's wall to bed, me
With my money belt of Northern ice.
I found Eliot and he said yes

And sprang into a Holmes cab.
Boswell passed me in the fog
Going to visit Whistler who
Was with John Donne who had just seen
Paul Potts shouting on Soho Green.

Midnight. I hear the moon
Light chiming on St Paul's.

The City is empty. Night
Watchmen are drinking their tea.

The Fire had burnt out.
The Plague's pits had closed
And gone into literature.

Between the big buildings
I sat like a flea crouched
In the stopped works of a watch.

A NOTE TO THE DIFFICULT ONE

This morning I am ready if you are,
To hear you speaking in your new language.
I think I am beginning to have nearly
A way of writing down what it is I think
You say. You enunciate very clearly
Terrible words always just beyond me.

I stand in my vocabulary looking out
Through my window of fine water ready
To translate natural occurrences
Into something beyond any idea
Of pleasure. The wisps of April fly
With light messages to the lonely.

This morning I am ready if you are
To speak. The early quick rains
Of Spring are drenching the window-glass.
Here in my words looking out
I see your face speaking flying
In a cloud wanting to say something.

TO MY WIFE AT MIDNIGHT

Are you to say goodnight
And turn away under
The blanket of your delight?

Are you to let me go
Alone to sleep beside you
Into the drifting snow?

Where we each reach,
Sleeping alone together,
Nobody can touch.

Is the cat's window open?
Shall I turn into your back?
And what is to happen?

What is to happen to us
And what is to happen to each
Of us asleep in our places?

2

I mean us both going
Into sleep at our ages
To sleep and get our fairing.

They have all gone home.
Night beasts are coming out.
The black wood of Madron

Is just waking up.
I hear the rain outside
To help me to go to sleep.

Nessie, dont let my soul
Skip and miss a beat
And cause me to fall.

3

Are you asleep I say
Into the back of your neck
For you not to hear me.

Are you asleep? I hear
Your heart under the pillow
Saying my dear my dear

My dear for all it's worth.
Where is the dun's moor
Which began your breath?

4

Ness, to tell you the truth
I am drifting away
Down to fish for the saithe.

Is the cat's window open?
The weather is on my shoulder
And I am drifting down

Into O can you hear me
Among your Dunsmuir Clan?
Are you coming out to play?

5

Did I behave badly
On the field at Culloden?
I lie sore-wounded now

By all activities, and
The terrible acts of my time
Are only a distant sound.

With responsibility
I am drifting off
Breathing regularly

Into my younger days
To play the games of Greenock
Beside the sugar-house quays.

6

Nessie Dunsmuir, I say
Wheesht wheesht to myself
To help me now to go

Under into somewhere
In the redcoat rain.
Buckle me for the war.

Are you to say goodnight
And kiss me and fasten
My drowsy armour tight?

My dear camp-follower,
Hap the blanket round me
And tuck in a flower.

Maybe from my sleep
In the stoure at Culloden
I'll see you here asleep

In your lonely place.

IMPLEMENTS IN THEIR PLACES

Somewhere our belonging particles
Believe in us. If we could only find them.

Who calls? Don't fool me. Is it you
Or me or us in a faulty duet
Singing out of a glade in a wood
Which we would never really enter?

This time the muse in the guise
Of jailbait pressed against
That cheeky part of me which thinks
It likes to have its own way.
I put her out and made her change
Her coarse disguise but later she came
Into the room looking like an old
Tinopener and went to work on the company.

One night after punching the sexual
Clock I sat where I usually sit
Behind my barrier of propped words.
Who's there I shouted. And the face
Whitely flattened itself against
The black night-glass like a white pig

And entered and breathed beside me
Her rank breath of poet's bones.

5

When I was a buoy it seemed
Craft of rare tonnage
Moored to me. Now
Occasionally a skiff
Is tied to me and tugs
At the end of its tether.

6

He has been given a chair in that
Timeless University.
The Chair of Professor of Silence.

7

My father's ego sleeps in my bones
And wakens suddenly to find the son
With words dressed up to kill or at
The least maim for life another
Punter met in the betting yard.

8

He cocked his snoot, settled his cock,
Said goodbye darling to his darling,
Splurged on a taxi, recited the name
Of his host and wondered who would be there
Worthy of being his true self to.

They were out. It was the wrong night.
By underground he returned home
To his reading darling saying darling
Halfway there I realised the night
Would have been nothing without you there.

9

She stepped from the bath, interestedly
Dried herself not allowing herself
To feel or expect too much. She sat
Not naked doing her face thinking
I am a darling but what will they think
When I arrive without my darling.
Moving in her perfumed aura,
Her earrings making no sound,
She greets her hostess with a cheek-kiss
And dagger. Then disentangled
She babys her eyes and sends her gaze
Widening to wander through
The sipping archipelagoes
Of frantic islands. He was there
It was their night. Groomed again
She lets herself in at four with an oiled
Key thinking my handsome darling
Is better than me, able to pull
Our house and the children round him.

10

Out into across
The morning loch burnished
Between us goes the flat
Thrown poem and lands
Takes off and skips One

[96]

2, 3, 4, 5, 6, 7, 8, 9,
And ends and sinks under.

11

Mister Montgomerie. Mister Scop.
You, follicles. You, the owl.
Two famous men famous for far
Apart images. POLEEP POLEEP
The owl calls through the olive grove.
I come to her in a set-in bed
In a Greenock tenement. I see
The little circle of brown moles
Round her nipple. Good Montgomerie.

12

I could know you if I wanted to.
You make me not want to.
Why does everybody do that?

13

Down in a business well
In a canyon in lower Manhattan
I glanced up from the shades
To see old dye-haired Phoebus
Swerving appear in his gold
Souped-up convertible.

14

The greedy rooks. The Maw
Of the incongruous deep.

The appetite of the long
Barrelled gun of the sea.
The shrew's consumption.
And me abroad ahunting
Those distant morsels
Admired by man.

15

Raped by his colour slides her delighted
Pupils fondled their life together.
It was the fifty dirty milkbottles
Standing like an army turned their love sour.

16

Failures of love make their ghosts
Which float out from every object
The lovers respectively have ever
Sighed and been alive towards.

17

Sign me my right on the pillow of cloudy night.

18

In my task's husk a whisper said
Drop it It's bad It's bad anyhow.
Because I could not gracefully
Get out of what I was doing, I made
An inner task come to fruit
Invisible to all spectators.

The fine edge of the wave expects.
Ireland Scotland England expects.
He She They expect. My dear
Expects. And I am ready to see
How I should not expect to ever
Enfold her. But I do expect.

So sleeps and does not sleep
The little language of green glow
Worms by the wall where the mint sprouts.
The tails the tales of love are calling.

When you were younger and me hardly
Anything but who is in me still
I had a throat of loving for you
That I can hardly bear can bear.

I see it has fluttered to your hand
Drowned and singed. Can you read it?
It kills me. Why do you persist
In holding my message upsidedown?

Ho Ho Big West Prevailer,
Your beard brushes the gable
But tonight you make me sleep.

24

It is how one two three each word
Chose itself in its position
Pretending at the same time
They were working for me. Here
They are. Should I have sacked them?

25

At times a rare metaphor's
Fortuitous agents sing
Equally in their right.

26

Nouns are the very devil. Once
When the good nicely chosen verb
Came up which was to very do,
The king noun took the huff and changed
To represent another object.
I was embarrassed but I said something
Else and kept the extravert verb.

27

Only now a wordy ghost
Of once my firmer self I go
Floating across the frozen tundra
Of the lexicon and the dictionary.

28

Commuting by arterial words
Between my home and Cool Cat

Reality, I began to seem
To miss or not want to catch
My road to one or the other. Rimbaud
Knew what to do. Or Nansen letting
His world on the wooden Fram freeze in
To what was going to carry him.

29

These words as I uttered them
Spoke back at me out of spite,
Pretended to not know me
From Adam. Sad to have to infer
Such graft and treachery in the name
Of communication. O it's become
A circus of mountebanks, promiscuous
Highfliers, tantamount to wanting
To be servant to the more interesting angels.

30

Language, constrictor of my soul,
What are you snivelling at? Behave
Better. Take care. It's only through me
You live. Take care. Don't make me mad.

31

How are we doing not very well?
Perhaps the real message gets lost.
Or is it tampered with on the way
By the collective pain of Alive?

Member of Topside Jack's trades,
I tie my verse in a true reef
Fast for the purpose of joining.

Do not think you have to say
Anything back. But you do
Say something back which I
Hear by the way I speak to you.

As I hear so I speak so I am so I think
You must be. O Please Please No.

Language, you terrible surrounder
Of everything, what is the good
Of me isolating my few words
In a certain order to send them
Out in a suicide torpedo to hit?
I ride it. I will never know.

I movingly to you moving
Move on stillness I pretend
Is common ground forgetting not
Our sly irreconcilabilities.

37

Dammit these words are making faces
At me again. I hope the faces
They make at you have more love.

38

There must be a way to begin to try
Even to having to make up verse
Hoping that the poem's horned head
Looks up over the sad zoo railings
To roar whine bark in the characteristic
Gesture of its unique kind.
Come, my beast, there must be a way
To employ you as the whiskered Art
Object, or great Art-Eater
Licking your tongue into the hill.
The hunter in the language wood
Down wind is only after your skin.
Your food has stretched your neck too
Visible over the municipal hedge.
If I were you (which only I am)
I would not turn my high head
Even to me as your safe keeper.

39

Why should I hang around and yet
Whatever it is I want to say
Delays me. Am I greedier than you?
I linger on to hope to hear
The whale unsounding with a deep
Message about how I have behaved.
Down under in the indigo pressures
He counts the unsteady shriek of my pulse.

40

Kind me (O never never).
I leave you this space
To use as your own.
I think you will find
That using it is more
Impossible than making it.
Here is the space now.
Write an Implement in it.

YOU ....

YOU ....

YOU ....

YOU ....

Do it with your pen.
I will return in a moment
To see what you have done.
Try. Try. No offence meant.

41

I found her listed under Flora
Smudged on a coloured, shining plate
Dogeared and dirty. As for Fauna
We all are that, pelted with anarchy.

42

Your eyes glisten with wet spar.
My lamp dims in your breath. I want
I want out of this underword
But I can't turn round to crawl back.

43

Here now at the Poetry Face
My safety lamp names the muse Mineral.

44

Brushing off my hurts I came across
A thorn of Love deeply imbedded.
My wife lent me her eye-brow tweezers
And the little bad shaft emerged.
It is on the mantel-piece now but O
The ghost of the pain gives me gyp.

45

Tonight late alone, the only
Human awake in the house I go
Out in a foray into my mind
Armed with the language as I know it
To sword-dance in the halls of Angst.

46

By night a star-distinguisher
Looking up through the signed air.
By day an extinguisher of birds
Of silence caught in my impatient
Too-small-meshed poet's net.

47

Under his kilt his master
Led him to play the fool
Over the border and burn
A lady in her tower
In a loud lorry road
In tulipless Holland Park.

It is only when the tenant is gone
The shell speaks of the sea.

Knock knock. I knock on the drowned cabin
Boy's sea-chest. Yearning Corbiere
Eases up the lid to look out
And ask how is the sea today.

I dive to knock on the rusted, tight
Haspt locker of David Jones.
Who looks out? A mixed company.
Kandinsky's luminous worms,
Shelley, Crane and Melville and all
The rest. Who knows? Maybe even Eliot.

Hello. It's a pleasure. Is that a knowledge
You wear? You are dressed up today,
Brigit of early shallows of all
My early life wading in pools.
She lifts my words as a shell to hear
The Celtic wild waves learning English.

These words as they are (The beasts!)
Will never realise the upper
Hand is mine. They try to come

The tin-man with me. But now (I ask.)
Where do they think what do they think
They are now? The dear upstarts.

53

The word unblemished by the tongue
Of History has still to be got.
You see, Huntly, it is the way
You put it. Said Moray's Earl,
You've spoilt a bonnier face than your ain.
That's what he said when Huntly struck
The Scots iron into his face.

54

Officer myself, I had orders
To stay put, not to advance
On the enemy whose twigs of spring
Waved on their helmets as they less
Leadered than us deployed across
The other side of the ravine of silence.

55

From ventricle to ventricle
A sign of assumed love passes
To keep the organisation going.
Sometimes too hard sometimes too soft
I hear the night and the day mares
Galloping in the tenement top
In Greenock in my child brain.

56

Terrible the indignity of one's self flying
Away from the sleight of one's true hand.
Then it becomes me writing big
On the mirror and putting a moustache on myself.

57

There is no fifty-seven.
It is not here. Only
Freshwater Loch Thom
To paddle your feet in
And the long cry of the curlew.

58

Occasionally it is always night
Then who would hesitate to turn
To hope to see another face
Which is not one's own growing
Out of the heaving world's ship-wall?
From my bunk I prop myself
To look out through the salted glass
And see the school of black killers.
Grampus homes on the Graham tongue.

59

I've had enough said twig Ninety-thousand
Whispering across the swaying world
To twig Ninety-thousand-and-Fifty. This lack
Of communication takes all the sap
Out of me so far out. It is true.

They were on their own out at the edge
Changing their little live angles.
They were as much the tree as the trunk.
They were restless because the trunk
Seemed to never speak to them.
I think they were wrong. I carved my name
On the bark and went away hearing
The rustle of their high discussion.

60

I stand still and the wood marches
Towards me and divides towards
Me not to cover me up strangled
Under its ancient live anchors.
I stand in a ride now. And at
The meeting, dusk-filled end I see
(I wish I saw.) the shy move
Of the wood's god approaching to greet me.

61

You will observe that not one
Of those tree-trunks has our initials
Carved on it or heart or arrow
We could call ours. My dear, I think
We have come in to the wrong wood.

62

In Madron Wood the big cock rook
Says CHYUCK CHYUCK if I may speak
Here on behalf of our cock members,
This year we're building early and some
Of us have muses due to lay.

Feeding the dead is necessary.

I love you paralysed by me.
I love you made to lie. If you
Love me blink your right eye once.
If you don't love me blink your left.
Why do you flutter your just before
Dying dear two eyes at once?

Cretan girl in black, young early
Widow from stark Malia, please have
The last portion and let your mask
Go down on the handkerchief dancing floor.
It's me that's lost. Find me and put
Me into an octopus jar and let me
Be left for the young spectacled
Archaeologist sad in a distant womb.

I caught young Kipling in his pelmanic
Kimsgame scribbling on his cuff.
I found he was only counting the beasts
Of empire still abroad in the jungle.

Coming back to earth under my own
Name whispered by the under dear,

I extracted with care my dead right arm,
An urchin of pins and needles of love.

68

The earth was never flat. Always
The mind or earth wanderers' choice
Was up or down, a lonely vertical.

69

The long loch was not long enough.
The resident heron rose and went
That long length of water trailing
Its legs in air but couldn't make it.
He decided to stay then and devote
Himself to writing verse with his long
Beak in the shallows of the long loch-side.

70

(Is where you listen from becoming
Numb by the strike of the same key?)
It is our hazard. Heraklion, listen.

71

I can discern at a pinch you
Through the lens of the ouzo glass,
Your face globing this whole Piraeus
Taverna of buzzing plucked wires.
Here we are sitting, we two
In a very deep different country

At this table in the dark.
Inevitable tourists us,
Not in Scotland sitting here
In foreign shadows, bouzouki
Turning us into two others
Across the waiting eating table.
At home in Blantyre if your mother
Looked at the map with a microscope
Her Scotch palate would be appalled
To see us happy in the dark
Fishing the legs of creature eight
Out of the hot quink ink to eat.

72

I am not here. I am not here
At two o'clock in the morning just
For fun. I am not here for something.

73

Of air he knows nor does he speak
To earth. The day is sailing round
His heavenly wings. Daisies and cups
Of butter and dragonflies stop
Their meadow life to look up wondering
How out of what ridiculous season
The wingèd one descends.

74

Somewhere our belonging particles
Believe in us. If we could only find them.

W. S. Graham is a Greenock man born in 1918.
He served his time as an engineer.
His first book of verse came out in 1942,
Cage Without Grievance.
After that came *The Seven Journeys* (1944),
2nd Poems (1945), *The White Threshold* (1949),
The Nightfishing (1955).
Malcolm Mooney's Land (1970).
Implements in Their Places (1977).
W. S. Graham has given readings of his verse in
England and in America, and has lectured at New York
University. He was given an Atlantic Award for
Literature in 1947.
His last two books were Poetry Book Society Choices
[England].
He is married to Nessie Dunsmuir from Blantyre
where David Livingstone came from and they
now live in Cornwall.